I

Ecumenical communities for people with learning disabilities

by

Helen Reid Thomas

All booklets are published thanks to the generous support of the members of the Catholic Truth Society

CATHOLIC TRUTH SOCIETY
PUBLISHERS TO THE HOLY SEE

Contents

Foreword

Our world is in such upheaval. Our societies have become places of competition where other people are seen only as rivals and where weakness is regarded only as a nuisance. In such a setting, people with disabilities are quickly put aside and devalued. In our communities of L'Arche we share our lives together with people with disabilities. We want to honour and respect each other.

Jesus inspired the birth of L'Arche in 1964 as this society of competition and rivalry was developing. Why did God inspire the foundation of L'Arche at that time? In an age that highlights technology and the intellect, Jesus wants us to discover that it is the human heart, relationship, which is important. People who are weak and rejected are important. And Paul tells us that God has chosen those who are weak and foolish to confound the powerful and clever (*cf 1 Cor 1:21*). In this same letter Paul says that the weakest members of the church, those who are the least presentable, "are necessary and should be honoured". (*cf Cor 12:22-26*).

L'Arche wants to be a place where they are honoured. In the gospel of Luke Jesus tells us that if we eat with those who are poor, crippled, disabled and blind, then we are blest. L'Arche wants to be a place of blessing for those who come to live and eat with those who are disabled and thus become their friend.

L'Arche is of course not the only place where people with disabilities are honoured or where we can discover that if we become their friends, we will become more human and closer to God. Many wonderful people all over the world are discovering this gift in their own way and helping them to find their place in the church and in society.

I pray that this booklet may help many to discover what we are discovering in L'Arche: it is a privilege and a gift to become the friend of a person with disabilities. That does not mean that life is "cosy". Community life, like family life, is not always easy! But we know that that if we want to do something worthwhile and work together for justice and peace in our world, creating communities of compassion, it is a struggle - a struggle that is truly worthwhile, a struggle through which the incredible power of the gospels and the love of Jesus are revealed to us.

I am grateful to Helen Reid Thomas for this booklet on L'Arche.

Jean Vanier,
Founder of L'Arche.

L'Arche

Introduction

It's 4 o'clock. Ingrid is finishing a complicated piece of tapestry, glancing every now and then at her pattern and counting her stitches. She has been working on it for months, very slowly but very accurately. She decided not to go to her day centre this morning and has spent a quiet day at home. Gordon has just arrived home in the Social Work bus. Anita, who has been waiting for his arrival, has watched him put down his bag, settle himself in his usual chair and take the usual can of Diet Coke out of his bag, before asking him about his day. Gordon is a man of routine. Brendan has been shopping and arrives home with bulging bags. "Hiya pal", says Gordon, holding out a friendly hand. The next to arrive is Tom, full of excitement about his visit with Pat to the Bird Centre in a nearby town. He communicates with signs and gestures and loud vocalisations as he is profoundly deaf and cannot speak. He tells his story to each person in turn and each responds in their own way. He settles down at the table to draw the birds he has seen. A couple of others drift in. Nicola goes to the kitchen to help Brendan with the cooking. It's Wednesday and in this house Wednesday evening is special, with a more elaborate meal than usual, followed by the house-meeting and then prayers for those who wish to take part. When we sit down to eat, we usually light a candle (Tom with his cigarette lighter is the officiant) and there is a bottle of wine and beer or cider to mark the special day. We hold hands to sing grace, then settle down to the serious work of eating.

So why bother with this description of what is in many ways a very ordinary occasion? What's different about this group of people? This is a house in one of the L'Arche communities in Britain, where a group of friends live together, sharing their home and their lives. Four of them are 'people with learning disabilities' and the others are, in L'Arche terminology, 'assistants'. Together they seek to create that mysterious thing called community.

Short history - The beginning

Founding stories are important. So often they seem in some way to anticipate the future of a movement. That is certainly the case with the founding story of L'Arche.

In 1964, a man called Jean Vanier was living in Paris. He was thirty-six years old, a Canadian, who had been in the navy during and after the war and had then become an academic, at one point holding the position of Professor of Moral Philosophy at the University of Toronto. He had a close friend, Pere Thomas Philippe, a Dominican priest, who was the chaplain of Val Fleuri, an institution housing about 30 men with mental handicaps, as they were then

Members of L'Arche Edinburgh celebrate the community's 10th birthday.

described, in the village of Trosly-Breuil. Pere Thomas very gently suggested to Jean that he might be able to begin 'something'. It was an opportune moment as there was a need for homes for such people and the French government was willing to give financial support. So Jean began to visit both Val Fleuri and other institutions and in one huge, forbidding asylum on the outskirts of Paris he got to know Philippe Seux and Raphael Simi. Both men had been placed in the asylum following the death of their parents.

Jean invited them to leave the institution in order to come and live with him in a small house he had bought in Trosly-Breuil, fifty miles north of Paris. In August 1964 they joined him and that was how L'Arche began.

At that stage Jean had no idea of setting up a new movement or that these beginnings would grow into the network of communities that now forms the International Federation of L'Arche. His concern was to discover how to live in community with Raphael and Philippe in that little house. He drew on the support of many friends, who gave their friendship, prayers, financial help and legal advice. He learned, as he has often said, a great deal about himself, about the foolishness of his own expectations and the demands and self-disciplines of true community life. In the early days, he asked a friend to suggest possible biblical names for the house. She suggested about a hundred without success but as soon as she said L'Arche, Jean knew that was the one. The name (meaning 'The Ark') has remained, with all its rich associations of the story of Noah and that first covenant made between God and the whole of humankind.

That first little house expanded more rapidly than anyone had expected. A few months after the opening, Jean was asked to take over the directorship of Val Fleuri, which housed over thirty men. The institution was in crisis, it was a huge responsibility and the future was uncertain, but, with the encouragement of Pere Thomas, Jean eventually agreed, believing that he was following God's call. So it happened that only a few months after its inception, L'Arche had become a body of more than fifty people, based in two houses. The overwhelming challenge was to discover how unity and community could be expressed in this new situation. Jean believes that it was through this experience that he was helped to discover the special gifts brought to the community by those members who were handicapped, and arising out of this, the specific vocation of L'Arche.

This vocation can be traced back to the story of the covenant God made with Noah, the representative of all humankind. The vision of L'Arche is inclusive. We are all individual persons made in the image of God and loved by God. No-one is outside this human family and each person has their own particular part to play in it. As a family we are diminished if we ignore the gifts of others. Too often the gifts of those with learning difficulties are ignored or passed over or are simply invisible in a society which values success and power above everything else.

Development in the world

L'Arche began in France, in a context where it was nourished first by the spiritual gifts of the Roman Catholic church. At its inception there was no thought of anything else: it was a simple local vision for a little group in a particular place. However, thanks to the people who were linked locally to that group and to those who heard about it through Jean's 'Letters to Friends', interest began to grow. Visitors came to share the life of the community and to help out in practical ways, and when they returned home they took something of the vision of L'Arche with them. Two further developments were particularly influential. Jean was invited to give a number of lectures and retreats, which brought many more people into contact with L'Arche and eventually inspired the foundation of new communities outside France. And in 1971 the first Faith & Light pilgrimage to Lourdes prepared the way for expansion in a new direction.

As Jean says, Faith & Light is 'like a first cousin to L'Arche' (*An Ark for the Poor:* 33). Its story originates in the desire of a French couple Gerard and Camille Proffit to take their two severely disabled children on pilgrimage to Lourdes. They received so little encouragement for the idea from the religious authorities that they decided to make the pilgrimage on their own. In Lourdes they were refused accommodation in the hotels. It was an experience of rejection and pain and they needed the support of friends. They told their story to Jean Vanier and a friend Marie Helene Matthieu. Over the next three years a pilgrimage was planned, specifically for families who had children with learning disabilities. On Holy Thursday 1971, twelve thousand people from fifteen countries came together to celebrate the pain of Good Friday and the joy of Easter Sunday. Out of this experience developed the network of Faith & Light communities, which bring together people with disabilities, their families and friends, to give each other support and to celebrate their lives. These are communities of people united by a common concern and shared experience but they are not residential. Faith & Light groups have by now spread to over seventy countries all over the world. While the value of this kind of support is immediately obvious, the emphasis on celebration may be more puzzling to the outsider. But this attitude of celebration lies at the heart of both Faith & Light and L'Arche: it is a joyful expression of delight in and gratitude for the tremendous individuality and the variety of gifts that the 'handicapped' enjoy and can offer to others. The attitude of celebration doesn't deny the reality of pain and anger and the daily practical problems experienced by people with disabilities and their families, but alongside and even through those experiences it finds hope and laughter and companionship and faith.

Meanwhile in Trosly and elsewhere in France, L'Arche was growing rapidly throughout the 1960s and 70s. Some of those who came to live in a L'Arche community had comparatively slight disabilities and were able to move into more independent living in their own apartments, to find jobs and in several cases to get married. Workshops were started to create employment for those who needed opportunities to do skilled work but in more supportive conditions than those generally available. There was no single pattern of a L'Arche house or a L'Arche community. As Jean describes it: 'We were doing things step by step; a house was for sale, we bought it and we filled it! We did not even ask if the house was properly adapted to the needs of those we were to welcome!'(*An Ark for the Poor:* 35)

Jean himself was away a good deal of the time, giving retreats and visiting other L'Arche foundations, so in time a Board of Directors was set up to provide a structure that would sustain the growing community in and around Trosly during his frequent absences. Pere Thomas continued to give his pastoral support and encouragement, and helped many people through what were potentially difficult or bewildering times. But it was also a time of great commitment and the sense of being part of something new and exciting was an inspiration to the assistants who came to Trosly from many different countries.

In the meantime L'Arche communities had been founded elsewhere. It was not perhaps surprising that one of the first communities to be set up outside France was near Toronto, as Jean had many family links with Canada (his father had been Governor General) and he visited Canadian churches and universities regularly. 'Daybreak' (known to many from the writings of Henri Nouwen) opened its doors in 1969. This was from the start an ecumenical community of Anglicans, Roman Catholics and Protestants. The other community that opened in 1969 may seem at first sight more surprising. This was in Southern India in the large city of Bangalore and the founder was a German woman, Gabrielle Einsle. The name it was given, Asha Niketan (Home of Hope), is now used for all the four Indian communities presently in existence, in Nandi Bazaar in the state of Kerala, in Chennai (as Madras is now known) and in Calcutta in addition to Bangalore. These communities have from the beginning included Hindus and Muslims as well as Christians. Similarly, a community founded five years later in Bouake in French-speaking West Africa, included Muslims and Animists among its earliest members. These communities have been from their beginning not only inter-church but inter-faith communities. The implications of these developments for L'Arche as a whole were enormous; the experience of L'Arche in India in particular has been radical in compelling the whole movement to reflect on the nature of its vocation and the ways of expressing this vocation in widely differing cultural and religious contexts. We shall look at these implications in more detail in a later section, which considers the spirituality of L'Arche.

L'Arche communities have continued to spring up all over the world and at the time of writing there are 117 communities in 31 countries as diverse as Japan and Honduras, Haiti and Poland. This diversity makes for a fascinating variety, more especially because a L'Arche community in any place takes its particular form from how people in that place live their particular national, cultural and religious identities. It also inevitably makes for tensions when people from such a variety of backgrounds try to forge some kind of commonality.

L'Arche in the UK

In 1971 Therese Vanier, Jean's sister, who was a consultant at St Thomas' Hospital in London, accompanied the Faith & Light pilgrimage to Lourdes. She spoke to her brother of the call she felt to start a L'Arche community in England and they agreed that if this was the will of God, some sign would be given as to what and where it should be. Soon afterwards, a house in Canterbury became available for purchase by L'Arche. Though in the end this possibility was not followed up, it directed Therese's thoughts towards that area of the country and finally, with the support of the Archbishop of Canterbury,

Michael Ramsey, an Anglican rectory was bought in Barfrestone in Kent. Therese, together with Ann and Geoffrey Morgan, made contact with a local hospital, where they met people who wanted to experience a different way of life by making a new home together. The community of L'Arche (Kent) was born in 1974 with the opening of Little Ewell, the first of its five houses.

The following year the second L'Arche community in the UK opened in Inverness. As with Little Ewell, the starting point was the offer of a property, on this occasion, a lovely old house near Loch Ness in the Highlands of Scotland, which was given outright to L'Arche. In the early spring of 1975, with the encouragement of Therese and Elizabeth Buckley, Ian Cameron, the first member of the community, left the hospital where he had lived for many years to begin a new way of life in Braerannoch.

In England, the founding of Little Ewell had been made possible by the support and active concern of members of the Anglican Church and the community included people from both Anglican and Roman Catholic traditions. Scotland presented a further ecumenical challenge, in that some of those who chose to live in L'Arche belonged to the Presbyterian tradition of the Church of Scotland. These experiences forced L'Arche to grapple with the question: what does it mean to live honestly and faithfully as an ecumenical community? What are the implications of such openness for the life and religious practice of the community? Though there are no easy answers, much thought and commitment has been given to these questions over the years and we will look at these in more detail later in this account.

At the time of writing there are eight L'Arche communities in the UK: in addition to Kent and Inverness, there are communities in London (Lambeth), Bognor Regis, Liverpool, Brecon, Edinburgh and most recently Preston. Most of the older foundations include workshops as well as several houses, reflecting the importance of giving dignity and value to work for people with learning disabilities. More recent communities have found they are able to cooperate with the better provision now available from local authorities, as these develop an increasingly 'person-centred' approach to the programmes they offer, and have therefore been less ready to start workshops of their own. Moreover, with the shift to 'care in the community' policies from government, big institutions have been broken up, and these days many members of L'Arche come not from long-stay hospitals but from their parental homes. This means that they already have a network of relationships in the wider social community which are important to them and which L'Arche seeks to sustain and develop further. The focus of these relationships is often the Adult Training Centre run by the local authority which the person has attended for years and this continuity is very important. In the UK, as elsewhere, L'Arche responds to the social and cultural changes that occur around it, changes which, indeed, it may have played a part in and influenced to some degree.

People sometimes ask: how does L'Arche begin in a particular place? A L'Arche community is not 'planted' as part of an overall plan of campaign at national or international level; rather, it grows out of local need, interest, desire and waiting in prayer. A small group of people may wait many years in hope before the moment seems right to establish a house: there must be a clear sense that a L'Arche house is really needed and wanted in that place, sufficient commitment locally to sustain it in its beginning and support it for the future, and an empowering awareness of God's guidance for the undertaking. At present in a number of places there are small 'seed groups' waiting and praying for the right moment to establish a community in their locality. In many instances, the initial interest has developed out of a visit from Jean Vanier or some other long-term member of L'Arche, or through someone attending a retreat organised by L'Arche and Faith & Light.

There are good reasons, born of experience, for this gradualist approach. Some of the earlier communities had to close for lack of local support; some were perhaps based too much on the vision and enthusiasm of one or two individuals, who then felt themselves called to another vocation elsewhere; some were in an isolated locality and could not find enough assistants to maintain the life of the house. It is not easy to sustain a community of this kind and while risk will always be part of the way of life in L'Arche, the willingness to entertain risk has to be balanced by a willingness to accept responsibility for the lives of those who come to live in L'Arche.

L'Arche structures

As L'Arche communities grew and multiplied all over the world, it became increasingly apparent that some kind of structure was needed to link these very diverse little groups in a wider relationship. In 1972 the founders of all the existing communities met at Ambleteuse, in France, where they prepared the first 'International Charter', which specifically addressed the Christian communities of L'Arche. The community in Bangalore (India), which was represented at this meeting, had already written its own charter, reflecting the particular concerns of interfaith communities, and many found it difficult to accept that the international family of L'Arche should have two distinct charters. Partly in response to these concerns, and partly to acknowledge the changing social and cultural contexts which the communities experience, the International Charter has been revised over the years; the current version, which is accepted by every community worldwide, can be found at the end of this booklet. Its first fundamental principle is this:

> Whatever their gifts or limitations, people are all bound together in a common humanity. Everyone is of unique and sacred value, and everyone has the same dignity and the same rights. The fundamental rights of each person include the rights to life, to care, to a home, to education and to work. Also, since the deepest need of a human being is to love and be loved, each person has a right to friendship, to communion and to a spiritual life.

The communities are called to unity:

> Unity is founded on the covenant of love to which God calls all the community members. This implies welcome and respect for differences. Such unity presupposes that the person with a learning disability is at the centre of community life.
>
> ...Home life is at the heart of a L'Arche community. The different members of a community are called to be one body. They live, work, pray and celebrate together, sharing their joys and their suffering and forgiving each other, as in a family.

That first meeting of the federation brought together members of six communities; at the third meeting in 1975, twenty-six communities were represented, while five hundred people from a hundred communities participated in the seventh meeting in 1994, when the present Charter was approved.

The international structures of L'Arche have developed gradually in response to need and are open to change where circumstances require it. At present, each community has a leader, almost always someone who has lived in L'Arche for some time. He or she is supported by the local committee. At the next level, there are Regional Coordinators, who support perhaps five or six communities in their region, and enable them to make links with one another and with communities beyond their own group. These regions are part of the so-called Zones, each with a leader who coordinates the work of that zone and represents it at international meetings. Those members of L'Arche with learning difficulties who want to share in the planning and organisation of their own houses and communities are increasingly doing so and they also participate in regional and international gatherings.

How L'Arche Works

Shared homes

A typical L'Arche house is a home shared by a group of people, some of whom have learning disabilities. It is different from many 'group-home' models in that the people in the house choose, insofar as they are able, to live together rather than alongside each other, disabled and assistants together. The analogy is with a family home rather than supported accommodation for individuals with disabilities. This way of living doesn't suit everyone; some may give it a try and decide eventually that it is not for them. People's needs may change. In the older communities, there are a few who, having lived quite comfortably in a shared house for some time, have decided to move to a more independent and private way of living, perhaps to their own flat near a community house. They continue to be supported by L'Arche and remain members of the community. Such a move is exciting and challenging, to both individual and community. Carol from L'Arche Erie, Pennsylvania, is someone who has chosen to go along this road. She described her development to a group of university students to whom she was giving a talk. She had come to L'Arche from a large psychiatric hospital and for many years 'she would not look in the mirror. She told us "I will not look in the mirror because I hate myself." After living some years in the community, after finding meaningful work, after joining a church and after learning to live with a friend in her own apartment, Carol decided one day to look in the mirror. "Do you know what I said?" she asked the group of students. "I looked at myself for the first time in many, many years and I said, You know, Carol, you don't look so bad after all!" (*Letters of L'Arche December 1996:5*)

When L'Arche began in Trosly, one of the problems was the lack of available models for this kind of community. Yet this has also been a source of power and freedom. Several developments of that time had elements in common. There were religious communities such as the Missionaries of Charity and Taize, which used traditional models of religious communities as a basis for their own vocation. There were, in the USA in particular, many small idealistic communes which were founded at that time in reaction to the assumptions of mainstream society. And, in some areas of Europe and in the US and Canada, professionally run group-homes for people with disabilities were being set up, inspired by the concept of 'normalisation': that is, integrating those with disabilities into ordinary society by as far as possible making available to them the normal opportunities and choices that are on offer to others.

Each of these models had something of value to offer and something in common with the new phenomenon of L'Arche. Even today L'Arche communities may resemble one or other of these models, according to context, and awareness of the tension between these different possibilities continues to be a source of open self-examination and debate within the International Federation. But as long as the basic L'Arche model continues to be the very simple one of a group of people making a home together, it remains enormously flexible. It can adapt to a highly organised and prescriptive social welfare system such as we find in France or the UK; it can work in the voluntary sector of the USA; it can manage, precariously it is true, in countries such as Haiti or India where there is no state provision and little voluntary organisation, but much reliance on friendship and individual generosity. The simplicity of its essential vision has given L'Arche the gift of freedom; the unity that lies at its heart enables its many varieties to flourish.

Let us turn again to that image we began with: that small group of people spending the evening together in their home.

Since this is Wednesday, everyone who belongs to the house is here for the evening. Core-members and assistants have all been doing different things during the day. Gordon has been to his beloved Adult Training Centre, which he has attended with hardly a break for the last twenty years. Today he was at a music group where he played the drums. He has very few words but is an outgoing, friendly character, someone who inspires great affection. Ingrid needs a lot of time on her own to process life so she stayed quietly at home today instead of going to her Centre. She doesn't initiate speech but she understands much of what is said and will respond. She and Jo, an English assistant, who is now in her second year in the community, have been putting her most recent photographs into an album and talking about them, remembering the occasions when they were taken. Anita, recently returned from a visit to her family in Hungary, has been working on the medication audit in preparation for the annual visit from the Social Work Registration Officer. She sits by Gordon and chats to him about his day. Brendan, from Australia, is doing the cooking with Nicola, who has very recently joined the community from her parents' home. She, like Gordon, is a sociable person and has spent a lively day at her Centre. Mandy, an assistant from former East Germany, a professional artist, is talking to Helen, the houseleader, about an exhibition of artwork by various members of L'Arche to celebrate the 10th anniversary of this little community. Tom, who has been at the bird-centre, has several paintings in the exhibition. He is now in his late fifties and has in many ways outgrown what his Day Centre has to offer. L'Arche has organised work provision to meet his particular needs, which includes some one-to-one sessions with Pat, a religious sister, who has retired from teaching and now helps part-time at L'Arche.

After the meal and the lively business of washing-up, with its regularly repeated comic routines, mostly instigated by Gordon, we return to the table for the house meeting. In this house, everyone communicates in a different way and it is vitally important that we all know and understand what is going on and what is going to happen in the week ahead. Without this attention to communication, there can be major misunderstandings and much distress and confusion. We look at the diary together and talk about what is coming up during the week ahead in the community, in the house and for each individual. As we talk, the houseleader draws a big calendar depicting the events of the coming week, with each person's activities represented on it in symbolic form. Meanwhile, with an assistant to help, each core-member makes their own calendar, mostly using the symbols, but in Ingrid's case writing it all out with great care. At the end of the meeting, the big calendar is ceremoniously hung on the wall and remains there as a reference point for the rest of the week. Gordon has earlier put out his drums, in preparation for prayers. Tom fetches his harmonica, we light the candle and settle into our time of prayer.

This Wednesday evening brings together several strands in the life of a L'Arche community. Most importantly, we gather together in friendship for a meal. We give God thanks for that meal and our time together. We share the tasks of cooking, laying and clearing the table, and washing up. We share, too, the discussion and planning of the next week's events. We pray together. And we relax, watching television or kicking a football in the garden. And woven in with all this and underpinning it is a highly professional attention to the needs of those with disabilities. In L'Arche we work closely with community health professionals, the doctors, nurses, psychologists and others. Detailed care plans are drawn up for each core-member and revised regularly, covering matters of nursing care, monitoring of outbursts, diet, social relationships and day provision. Diaries are kept for each person, recording anything that may be significant. None of the core-members in this house is able to manage their own finances so these too have to be managed and recorded faithfully.

Everyone in a L'Arche community has an annual review. Where assistants are concerned, this will involve the Community Leader or Assistants' Coordinator and the Houseleader. For the core-members, more people are involved: family and friends, the keyworker from the Day Centre, the community nurse, possibly a social worker, in addition to members of the L'Arche community. It's a big event and one that people look forward to and prepare for with feeling and thought and imagination. For some people it's a time when they consider very carefully their continuing commitment to the community and they may discuss it with many friends before coming to a decision. At a recent review the person concerned was someone who finds it very difficult to initiate speech so she prepared for the review by choosing a few objects that would represent what had been important for her in the previous year: a tapestry that she had completed and had shown in an exhibition; the 'memory box' that she started while she was taking part in bereavement counselling; her album of photographs detailing significant events, holidays, her move to a new Day Centre, birthdays, and so on. With support, she was able to lead the first part of the meeting. The people there gave their feedback and their observations. Together the group looked at the goals from last year, the extent to which these had been achieved and their continuing relevance, and considered the new goals, to which the person concerned had given her input in the planning of the review.

The willingness to draw on professional expertise has been a feature of L'Arche from very early on, when a psychiatrist gave regular support to the new community in Trosly. It would be irresponsible to neglect this element of the vocation of L'Arche, which is to give the highest possible standard of care in all respects. Moreover, these relationships in the wider social network provide continuity and friendship for both core-members and assistants. The community nurse may well have known a particular person for years, far longer than anyone in L'Arche; she holds that person's story and is able to help and advise a new assistant with the benefit of her knowledge in a way that no-one else can. Over the years she becomes a true friend of the community and is given a great welcome when she arrives for her regular visit.

In the present climate of change in the provision of social services in the UK, L'Arche is being required to consider carefully a whole range of issues, from the standard of physical accommodation to the training of assistants. This is very demanding but also good for us; it forces us to think carefully about our present structures, recruitment and training procedures and to question aspects of our patterns of work. The challenge that faces us is to find a way to reconcile these rigorous statutory requirements with the mutuality and spontaneity that lie at the heart of our way of living in L'Arche. As Jean Vanier says, 'What characterises L'Arche is the union of three aspects: the spiritual, the 'living together' and the professional - if any one were missing, we would no longer be L'Arche.'

The local L'Arche community

A L'Arche community generally consists of two to five houses, an office, and perhaps a couple of workshops or a horticultural project. The houses are wherever possible within walking distance of one another and there is a good deal of informal coming and going between them. On a more formal level, the whole community meets about once a month for a Community Gathering. At this gathering there will be members of the houses and also other friends attached to L'Arche, perhaps former assistants who live nearby and come with their children, or members of the committee and support group, perhaps a local priest or minister. This is a time for informal meeting and also for worship together and the exchange of news, followed by a shared meal. The presence of families with children in L'Arche is important as many of the core-members love babies and children but have little opportunity to get to know them in their day-to-day life. It's a delight to see particular relationships fostered in this way.

L'Arche lays much emphasis on welcome and hospitality. Some people have a great gift for this and are eager to invite almost everyone they meet to visit their home. Some core-members enjoy having visitors but are not able to initiate invitations themselves and need help to do so. Others are more reticent or fragile and need to be gently protected from too much disruption of their normal routine. Maintaining a balance between openness and reassurance can be a delicate operation.

Links with other L'Arche communities are valuable and are developed through visits of pairs or groups and exchanges of assistants for short periods. The summer holidays also provide an opportunity for making links, in that a group from Dublin, for example, may do a house exchange with the community in Preston or Inverness.

Links with the wider social community

The core-members who came to live in L'Arche fifteen or twenty years ago in Britain, and generally in European countries, were likely to have a history of institutional living, and consequently fairly narrow horizons of contact and friendship. In these circumstances, L'Arche provided a home, a place of work and much of their social life. In the newer communities, most people who choose to live in L'Arche come from their parental homes. They may come at any age between twenty and forty, but whenever it is they almost certainly have a number of established relationships in the wider community, with which they enrich the life of their new home. These will be with family members and friends from home, people in their workplace or day-centre, clubs (which may include Faith & Light) and other activities. Some have church links, which they may want to maintain. In most cases it is the responsibility of assistants to make sure that these relationships are fostered because they provide continuity between the different parts of the individual's life and preserve those shared memories, which are so crucial for the sense of self. At the same time, new contacts will gradually open up with neighbours, shopkeepers, the GP, the local church. This sense of being part of a wider community is very important in L'Arche. Though the house does provide a necessary haven, it is not in any way a ghetto or a place of escape from the world. Some people with learning disabilities have a great gift for making friendships. Walk out on the streets of Leith with Gordon or George and you will find yourself greeting half the local population. They give new assistants a wonderful introduction to the place.

The value of the more formal links with the professional services has already been noted. Psychologists, psychiatrists and health specialists provide ongoing insight and support for people with special difficulties such as autism or challenging behaviour or Alzheimer's Disease. Friendly links with keyworkers in day-centres are tremendously valuable for knowing how people get on outside the home environment. For the new assistant, too, making these links can be a way of broadening their own contacts.

Links with churches

L'Arche is open to members of any Christian church, to those who belong to other faith traditions and also to those with no religious affiliation. However, the majority of those who belong to L'Arche in the UK have links with a church. Church congregations have become increasingly welcoming and outgoing towards people with learning difficulties in recent years, in some places because of the presence of L'Arche members. People with learning disabilities who wish to be full members of their church are now welcomed to communion, which was not always the case.

It can be a deeply moving experience to share in worship with a friend who has learning disabilities. I can think of a recent occasion when friends from L'Arche came to my mother's funeral. My sister told me that at the beginning of the service she was anxious and on edge but when in the first hymn she heard a wonderful, if not always tuneful, voice vigorously upraised in song behind her, she felt her tensions vanish and she could relax and really share in the service. We go regularly from our L'Arche house to an evening service with someone who cannot speak but who enters so profoundly into the prayer of stillness and silence during the time of meditation that whoever is with her is also drawn into that depth.

Funding in L'Arche

L'Arche is funded in each country according to the laws and customs of that country. Governmental provision may be available or money may have to be raised, whether locally or internationally. In the UK, the government gives funding for residential and day provision of members with learning disabilities, covering the majority of day-to-day costs in each community. However, L'Arche has to fundraise for capital projects including buildings and equipment. In countries where there is neither governmental provision nor a strong tradition of voluntary support, new houses receive help through the International network of L'Arche from more established communities.

Assistants in L'Arche

From the earliest days in Trosly, people, especially young people, have been attracted by the life of L'Arche. Many want, of course, to be of use in some way, to give something of themselves to others; many are drawn by the notion of community; some have had experience of living with a brother or sister with learning disabilities; and there is also the excitement of doing something new and different, possibly in another country. There are British assistants in French communities, Polish and Czech in the UK, Ugandans in London, British in Bangalore - one of the great attractions of L'Arche is its international nature.

Many assistants come intending to live in the community for a year and they leave at the end of that time. Some choose to remain longer and of those a few stay on for many years, making L'Arche their long-term home. Occasionally, people in mid-career or nearing retirement choose to make a decisive move to a new kind of life in L'Arche. Jean and Therese Vanier and Henri Nouwen are among these and there are many others less well known. The community in Preston have a retired teacher among their assistants. My own move to L'Arche came after a number of years of work in a university. Those who remain in L'Arche do so because they are drawn to something in the life of the community which affects them at a profound level. They have moved beyond the stage of 'wanting to be useful' - though one would hope they continue to be so! - to the stage where they are able to acknowledge their own deep needs and experience the meeting of these needs through their relationships in the community.

For many assistants life in L'Arche can be extraordinarily busy. As Tim Kearney says: 'The dual identity of L'Arche as faith community and service provider for people with learning disabilities does indeed create a daunting workload and an intensity of life. While it enables the core members to enjoy a relaxed pace of life, it often calls assistants to assume a busy and demanding rhythm.' (*A Prophetic Cry:78*) There is a house to run, administrative tasks to be seen to, diaries and personal files for core members to be kept, health issues to follow up, community events to organise - the list goes on and on. Where core members need a great deal of physical care, that is both tiring and very time-consuming. On the other hand, where someone is able to take part in household tasks or wants to shop for their own clothes, accompanying them and giving support can be equally time-consuming. Learning to live at other people's pace is not easy. For older assistants, who have done what might be called 'ordinary jobs' before coming to L'Arche, learning to relax and to enjoy 'wasting time' with people is something they may have to work at quite hard! It is sometimes almost easier to revert to 'busyness' and the satisfying ticking off of tasks achieved. There is so often a tension between the desire simply to be with someone, sometimes doing nothing more than sitting in companionable silence or watching a video together, and the pressure to rush around trying to do all that has to be done.

In fact, it is those times of being together that make sense of the whole. That is where the spirituality of L'Arche is to be found even when there is no overtly religious expression of it; where two or three are together, simply to be with and for one another, there is our Lord in the midst of them. It's this that provides the nourishment for the rest of life.

When I agreed to write this account of L'Arche, I knew that it would be important to draw on the words of people with learning disabilities and assistants. I have used the words of core-members at various points but speech is not the chosen mode of communication for most people with learning disabilities. Gesture, expression and touch are often more significant and these unfortunately cannot be transferred to paper. However, I felt that a section specifically focused on what assistants feel and think would be of interest. I asked the Assistants' Coordinators in the UK communities to elicit contributions and received a number of extraordinarily interesting and often moving letters. There are a number of common areas and the quotes are presented in those contexts.

I asked assistants why they had decided to stay on in L'Arche beyond their initial commitment. The most significant reasons were that they had come to experience their L'Arche house and community as their home; that they felt valued and accepted; that they had made deep friendships with people with learning disabilities; that they believed in the value of the work they were doing; that in L'Arche they found an integrity of life, in which the social, emotional, spiritual and intellectual aspects of themselves were given room to grow.

Ann-Marie writes of L'Arche as home: 'Somewhere to rest my head, warmth, shelter, a comfy bed and a room to have time and space just for myself...More importantly...is that it has been and is the home of my heart. In L'Arche I have learned and still learn, to risk being myself, to risk being in relationship with myself, others and God - to risk loving and being loved.'

On friendship, Jane, who had previous experience of working with people with learning disabilities in a school, says L'Arche is 'a way of being with people with learning disabilities unlike any other, a place that changes people's lives...I was able to make the sort of relationships...that I was told not to do in other places. To be friends before being a carer. Have my friend worry about me when things were tough and delight in happy times with me, to share my life, I suppose.'

Baska wrote: 'The extreme busyness of community life sometimes is especially frustrating because, above all, for a relationship of true tenderness to develop, it takes time. It may only be when starting the second or third cup of tea that someone will ask: "How are you really? How are you, Baska?" And you know from the tone of the voice and the depth of that question going through your spine that you are being really seen and really cared for.'

Mary writes about emotional healing: 'The pain and anguish of disability may never be cured from a medical point of view, however I'm often struck by the almost tangible healing of emotional pain which takes place when we learn to trust, to listen, to love and respect each other. This often involves the painful process of addressing and re-addressing personal grief and loss. This ongoing process fosters acceptance (to some degree at least) which has tremendous power for healing and reconciliation.'

The sense of wholeness that L'Arche can nourish is expressed by many. Phil had been in L'Arche for a year, left at the end of that time with lots of questions, and then after post-graduate study and an extended period of travel, felt called to return. 'Returning to L'Arche for me was part of a wider homecoming that has been a big event in my life - coming home to the church, realising that everything I had left to find was already there - just not obviously so, like the treasure buried in the field.'

Helen left an academic job to become a house assistant because 'I was looking for integrity, a way of living in which different aspects of my own being...could come together. However clever the people might be that I had worked with for so many years, I was bored with dealing with such a narrow range of humanity. I wanted to be able to share and enjoy and feel deeply something of the variety and difference of human experience.'

Several tell of the sense that they are accepted as they are: 'Others have not run away from my vulnerabilities'(Ann-Marie); 'I have never felt so able to be myself anywhere and know I would be accepted, and that is from a non-Christian in a Christian community'(Jane).

L'Arche communities are very international in their mix of assistants. Fiona, an Australian, offers a comment from her experience on the freedom of choice that being away from home can offer: 'It was easier for me to do something "different", like L'Arche, in a foreign country. Had I been in my own country, I would have felt more obliged to get a "real job", I think.'

A recurring theme is the value of each individual as they are and for what they are. Maria, who is from Lambeth where they have recently experienced more than one death in the community, writes that: 'Each L'Arche member is appreciated and celebrated every year in a special way on their birthday and maybe most profoundly at the end of their life. For us as a community it has been very moving to experience the unity in caring and praying for a dying community member and the depth of joy and gratitude far beyond (and in spite of) the grief, the way we could say good-bye and celebrate the person's life. For me, that has been a real grace and I could not imagine a more beautiful way to die.'

Almost every assistant who wrote to me stressed the depth and value of the relationships that develops between those who lived together. The corollary of this is that it is very hard when assistants leave a community: hard for the assistants but perhaps even harder for those who remain behind and have to cope with the departure of a close and trusted friend. This is one of the very painful aspects of a shared life and while there is always some degree of continuity there is also an ever-present awareness of loss.

The 'language' of L'Arche

Every organisation develops its own codes of communication to some degree and L'Arche is no exception. English speakers have been known to find some of the vocabulary of L'Arche difficult and occasionally alienating. This difficulty arises in part from the history of the movement and its rooting in a specifically French and Roman Catholic linguistic, religious and cultural milieu. Many of the terms used are imported directly from French because precise equivalents do not exist in English. For example, there is 'accompaniment', which means providing assistants (and others) with the opportunity to meet regularly and confidentially with an experienced member of the community in a relationship which is distinct from both counselling and spiritual direction, though it may include elements of both; and 'formation', which includes both professional training and personal and spiritual development. Other commonly used terms, such as 'discernment', have a particular religious history, which may be unfamiliar to those from a different background.

There is also a significant use of language by which L'Arche distinguishes its own practice from the world of professional and client relationships. Because in a L'Arche home the emphasis is on mutuality and shared living, we do not talk about 'staff' or 'service users'. While everyone in the house is a member of L'Arche, some are members with learning disabilities, or 'core members', and some are 'assistants'. Assistants do not have rotas or duty times; but they do have times when they 'are around' and times when they are free. These may seem insignificant points to make but it is a fact that language does to some extent shape thought and our use of language both reflects and influences our thinking.

A third aspect of the language of L'Arche is related to the moment in history of its inception. L'Arche came into being during an extraordinarily creative period in Western cultural history. It was a time of many small and some large revolutions, a time when numerous young people in particular were seeking to explore different ways of being human, of living generously together in hospitality and community. It was also a period of creative theological exploration, through the work of the Second Vatican Council of the Roman Catholic Church and the development in many other churches of an incarnational theology proclaiming the key biblical concepts of justice, service and identification with the poor. The linguistic usage that was an inspiration and a call to so many at that time can still be heard in the way in which L'Arche expresses its vision and calling today. L'Arche publications still frequently use the terms 'the poor' and 'the weak'; the L'Arche prayer refers to the 'little ones'. There is indeed Scriptural support for the use of such language (e.g. Matthew 5:3-10, I Cor.1:23-29). And it is true, too, that these words challenge all who belong to L'Arche for, whether or not we have learning disabilities, we are led by the experience of our shared way of life to the acknowledgement that we are, each one of us, the 'poor' and the 'weak'. But I would suggest also that this is an area where we might allow ourselves to be challenged by the attention that is given to language use in contemporary society, with its emphasis on taking a positive view of people with physical or intellectual disabilities, as people first and foremost, who happen to have certain disabilities. We might also ask whether this way of talking about people with disabilities as 'the poor' and 'the weak' actually represents our daily experience of living in a L'Arche house or working in a workshop. How do the members of L'Arche who have learning disabilities wish to speak of themselves, or be spoken of? Does the language we use reflect our actual thinking and doing? How can we express what we do more clearly and convincingly? This is a challenge which some of our communities are engaging with at the present time.

Spirituality of L'Arche

The celebration of difference

L'Arche is founded upon the celebration of difference. When Jean Vanier invited Raphael Simi and Philippe Seux to share his home, he thought he would be in charge, he would be the helper and the organiser, the one who would bring gifts to this little group. His experience of living with them turned his expectations upside down. He learned to understand something of the pain of rejection that they had experienced, but he sensed also 'how living with them could transform me, not through awakening and developing my qualities of leadership and intelligence, but by awakening the qualities of my heart.' (*An Ark for the Poor:20*) Now when Jean Vanier speaks of 'the heart', he does not mean 'the emotions'. There is nothing sentimental in this. By 'the heart' he means that which is at the core of our being, which is deepest in each of us. In the adult world of pressure and responsibility, achievement and betrayal, we can lose that sense of our centre. We are conditioned into forms of self-presentation which disable us at deeper levels. Jean found that living with Raphael and Philippe helped him to discover his own self, the treasure hid in the field of his own being. They had gifts to offer him which he had simply been unaware of and he had to live with them to discover what these were.

L'Arche communities, indeed the individual houses, are rooted and grounded in difference: the difference between people with learning disabilities and assistants; men and women; old and young; Roman Catholic, Anglican, and Protestant; Hindu, Muslim and Jew; believers and non-believers; short-stay assistants and long-term members; different nationalities. No-one should minimise the tensions and the conflicts that can spring from these differences. Those are a real and significant part of most people's experience in L'Arche. But these differences are not obstacles to be avoided in our life together, they are not to be regretted or wished away. They are the stuff out of which our unity as human beings sharing a common life can grow and be strengthened. L'Arche celebrates the beauty of difference. In place of a narrowing concept of the 'norm', we seek in our life to assert and delight in the variety and abundance of what it is to be human. Where such difference is valued, it can be a great source of life, because people are allowed to be different, to be themselves rather than conforming to a pattern.

The issue of 'normalisation' is sometimes raised in this context, that is, the policy of encouraging people with disabilities to live an unsegregated life with, as far as possible, the same opportunities for experience as their contemporaries without disabilities. The theory of normalisation confronts us with important questions about the way things are done in our own communities. Is L'Arche sometimes in danger of being over-protective, even paternalistic? Does it tend to over-spiritualise people with disabilities, imposing some kind of redemptive function on them, blocking their progress as individuals? As far as is possible L'Arche is an open and democratic society, relying on the authority of relationships rather than the authority of a hierarchical structure. It is salutary for us to pay attention to the values of normalisation and to ensure that whatever is good in its practice and theory finds a place in the way our communities operate.

On the other hand, what are the assumptions that lie behind the theory of normalisation? Very crudely, that there is a norm or standard of what is human, and that we should accept society's judgement as to what that norm is, and aspire to it as far as possible. Most people in L'Arche would have questions about those assumptions, and so, probably, would many Christians outside L'Arche. Many also have strong reservations about the highly individualistic tendency of Western society, which may be fulfilling in certain ways and for certain people, but which can be desperately destructive for others. There are those, with or without disabilities, who find they can achieve their own individuated fullness only by experiencing the sharing and support of a community. We do care in L'Arche about people with learning disabilities having opportunities to live their lives as fully as possible, like their contemporaries. But we also value the differences of people with learning disabilities and the uniqueness of each person in the fullness of their individuality. One can no more generalise about those with learning disabilities than one can about any other group. But perhaps this much we can say, that for the most part their personalities have not been standardised and made to conform to social expectations in the way that has happened to the rest of us, and that freedom to be themselves is their special gift to our communities.

A L'Arche house is, in the words of an Iona Community song, a home 'inspired by love and anger, disturbed by need and pain'. It would be wrong to present L'Arche as a kind of cosy Utopia of love and forgiveness and hugs and happy songs. Those are indeed part of our life but at the heart of L'Arche we also know anger, need and pain. These powerful experiences cut across all the differences. The core members in L'Arche all have some learning disability - many have multiple disabilities, both intellectual and physical - which is their primary handicap. And most have what is sometimes called 'secondary handicap', which is far more disabling, that is, the pain of rejection, the sense of failing to meet expectations, the experience of one's difference as something negative. Not everyone carries this burden. Nick Ellerker, the subject of a book by Therese Vanier (*Nick: Man of the Heart*), seems to have been wonderfully free of it, and there are others like him who have been born into happy and accepting homes and given a confident sense of being loved for who they are. They are the lucky ones and they have an unselfconscious ease with others which makes them a blessing in any group. Others have been marked by the experience of early rejection and disappointment and this pain remains deep at the centre of their being. Some can express it only by way of aggressive and violent anger or self-mutilation or withdrawal into speechlessness. Others live in constant anxiety, asking questions, talking constantly, seeking reassurance that life will be manageable. Living with this pain and anger and anxiety is hard for other members of the community, including the assistants. It may make them feel inadequate in the face of such experiences. It can open up their own insecurities and make them, too, vulnerable to pain, anger and a sense of rejection. These experiences are not to be sought out, but neither are they to be avoided when they present themselves. They test both the individual and the community and they are at the heart of our shared life.

Ecumenism and L'Arche

The following section is based on Therese Vanier's book *One Bread One Body: the ecumenical experience of L'Arche*, which gives a full account of the evolving vocation of L'Arche as an ecumenical community. Anyone interested in finding out more should read her book.

> L'Arche communities are communities of faith, rooted in prayer and trust in God. They seek to be guided by God and by their weakest members, through whom God's presence is revealed. Each community member is encouraged to discover and deepen his or her spiritual life and live it according to his or her particular faith and tradition. Those who have no religious affiliation are welcomed and respected in their freedom of conscience. (*Charter of L'Arche III.I.I.*)

The ecumenical experience of L'Arche has been a product of its history. The founders of the movement did not set out to form ecumenical communities; the communities were formed in response to a need in a particular place and to the promptings of the Spirit. L'Arche is ecumenical not because this was the intention at its foundation but because in actuality its members come from and are rooted in different Church and Faith histories and L'Arche feels called to support people in their own traditions. Mel Kirzner, a Jewish member of L'Arche Daybreak, the L'Arche community in Ontario, had never had his Bar-Mitzvah. 'I've lived most of my life with Christians. I've never gone up to the Torah. When I was 13, the other boys had a Bar-Mitzvah, but I didn't.' (*Letters of L'Arche No.93 1997*) A few years ago, with the support of the L'Arche community, Mel celebrated his Bar-Mitzvah at the age of 54.

Pentecost 1998: Pope John Paul II with Jean Vanier, founder of L'Arche.

To recapitulate briefly: as Jean Vanier himself comments on L'Arche's beginnings in France "L'Arche's first seeds were planted in the earth of the Roman Catholic Church" (*Ark for the Poor p. 79*) and we continue to grow with its support locally, nationally and internationally . The next community opened in Canada, founded by an Anglican couple who had lived in Trosly. They were joined by members of Reformed churches and also by Roman Catholics. They welcomed members of all Christian traditions and those of other faiths to their community. A year later Asha Niketan was founded by Gabrielle Einsle, a German Roman Catholic, in Bangalore, India, where the majority of core members were of course Hindus. In 1974 the first community in Africa opened its doors. It was in Bouake, in French-speaking West Africa, and its members were predominantly from a Muslim or Animist background.

Thus, without consciously seeking to do so, L'Arche communities were bringing together people who were divided not only by intellectual difference, but also by culture and religious tradition. The ecumenical vocation of L'Arche springs out of this experience.

Eucharistic celebration in the communities

Soon after the opening of Daybreak, it became clear that the issue of celebration of the Eucharist in communities would be a potential minefield. The rules of the different churches are irreconcilable, based, as they are, on different theologies of what Communion is. In normal circumstances the Roman Catholic church does not permit intercommunion with members of churches other than the Orthodox. The Orthodox will not normally permit Christians of any other church to receive communion or allow its members to receive communion elsewhere. The Anglican church welcomes baptised Christians of other denominations to the Eucharist but neither Roman Catholics nor Orthodox are permitted by their own churches to accept the invitation. The World Alliance of Reformed Churches has a policy of 'the open table', since 'the table is the Lord's, not ours'. The traditional invitation at a communion service in the Church of Scotland (which is Reformed) is 'to all who love the Lord'.

The pain of exclusion is felt by members of all traditions in an ecumenical community. The common practice of offering a blessing where it is not permitted to receive communion is generally followed but it does not make the pain any less. And this kind of divisiveness at the Eucharist makes no sense at all to those with learning disabilities; the sense of rejection that they experience may, indeed, cause distress or anger. It is a pain shared by all. Therese Vanier writes of her own experience: 'Although I say 'we all share in the one bread', I must then ask to be blessed rather than sharing in the one bread. And I ask myself, Why do I go on saying these words? What is this bread which I share, yet do not share?' (*One Bread One Body:83*) It is important in this context to emphasise that L'Arche does not seek special treatment from the Churches, saying in effect 'poor us and poor people with learning disabilities who can't understand'. It is not a well-meaning concern for the welfare of those who cannot understand theological complexities that drives the ecumenical concern of L'Arche. Its ecumenical vocation springs rather from the living experience of community life and the particular gift of people with learning disabilities to require unity. The late Lord Runcie tells the story of a particular Eucharist which he celebrated at a L'Arche retreat. At that service 'there was a man called Robert ... A casual observer might have dismissed him as awkward and inarticulate. He presented himself in a line with those coming up for communion or a blessing. Robert seemed uncertain what he was asking for. Finally, he took the host, looked at it and then broke it in two and handed half of it back to me. There could have been no better expression of the truth that we are spiritually nourished not by the owning but the sharing of God's gift.' (*Foreword to Nick: Man of the Heart; xiv*)

In L'Arche a liturgy has developed from the story of Jesus' washing his disciples' feet at the Last Supper on the night before he died. The story is told by St John and in his gospel it is a parallel to the account of the institution of the Eucharist that is given by the other three gospel writers. It has become a deeply significant symbolic act for L'Arche in the UK. On Holy Thursday most communities celebrate the Passover meal together and the liturgy of washing the feet is associated with this. First the Gospel story is acted out by some of the members of the community and then in small groups people wash and anoint one another's feet in silence. This is done slowly and reverently and with gentleness. It is deeply moving experience. We are debarred from sharing the Eucharist but in washing one another's feet we are able to express both our unity and the mutuality of our relationships and over the years this liturgy has become a focal rite in our communities.

Belonging to our local churches

In most L'Arche communities people attend their own local church services on a Sunday, which may be Anglican, Roman Catholic, Church of Scotland, Baptist or other. It can still happen that a person with learning disabilities may be refused communion, but that is now happily a rare event. For most church membership means a great deal; it is an important aspect of their sense of self and a source of friendship and support. But the ecumenical nature of L'Arche can make considerable demands on assistants. In a house with four core members, people may belong to as many churches. Sunday morning can be quite a marathon as assistants help people get ready and accompany them each to their own church, often with the result that the assistants themselves are unable to attend the services of their own tradition.

In order to root L'Arche members more deeply in their parishes, the International Council of L'Arche has urged communities to appoint pastoral ministers to the community, who would support the community leader in his or her pastoral and spiritual responsibilities. In Roman Catholic communities, the local bishop is asked to nominate a priest or religious or in some cases a lay person to fulfil this role. In interdenominational communities church leaders of the different traditions are consulted. Local clergy and ministers may also give support to the community through their gift of spiritual accompaniment for individual assistants.

Engagement with Church structures

Every two years the executive of the International Council of L'Arche meets with church leaders from a number of countries, leaders who accompany our communities. In 1990 the Council issued a paper entitled 'The Place of Ecumenism in L'Arche'. This was revised and reissued in 1994. The Council takes the view that since each community is rooted in the culture and religious traditions of its particular situation, 'ecumenical problems' cannot be solved centrally. It therefore encourages individual communities to work closely with local churches and church leaders and with those of other faiths in their area.

In the UK a Pastoral Ecumenical Committee has been formed, which has proved to be of considerable value. It is accountable to the group of Church Leaders and Coordinators of L'Arche in the UK, and brings together representatives from each of the UK communities. The committee maintains contact with the ecumenical bodies of different churches and with members of the inter-church process 'Churches Together', as well as with the Association of Interchurch Families (a network which offers support for interchurch or 'mixed' marriages). In response to the expressed needs of communities papers have been produced on 'Healing a Wound' and 'Blessing at the Time of Communion'.

Great importance is attached to the ongoing relationship with the different churches and ecumenical instruments in a given country. However, L'Arche feels the need for a wider perspective as well because communities are so widespread. Therefore the executive of the International Council of L'Arche meets with church leaders of different denominations and from a number of countries where they are involved in the pastoral care of L'Arche communities. This is an opportunity to consider together the experience of communities and to ask questions and offer insights and advice. The executive also maintains regular contact with a group from the World Council of Churches and another group from the Anglican Communion, as well as committees of the Vatican who deal with matters relating to Lay Movements, to Unity among Christians and to Interfaith matters.

On the eve of Pentecost 1998 Pope John Paul II held an historic meeting with delegates to the World Congress of Ecclesial Movements and New Communities. This was organised by the Pontifical Council of the Laity. L'Arche was invited to send six delegates, which included a member of L'Arche-Haiti, a core member from Trosly and Jean Vanier. Jean was among the four founders who were asked to speak at the meeting.

In the previous year Jean had been invited to address the Central Committee of the World Council of Churches and after his talk those who were present shared the liturgy of washing one another's feet. When Jean was invited to the Lambeth Conference of the worldwide Anglican Communion in 1999 he led a similar liturgy. The wife of one of the bishops, who herself took part in the liturgy on that occasion, told me later that it was one of the most moving experiences of her life. A year later, in May 2000, Jean visited Scotland, where he addressed the General Assembly of ministers and elders of the Church of Scotland.

Prayer in L'Arche communities

In most communities there is a chapel or a prayer room, often more than one. Some are used mainly for the celebration of the Eucharist; others primarily for private contemplative or small group prayer.

In the first community of Trosly there is a large chapel, but also a small oratory, where the Blessed Sacrament is reserved and exposed regularly. This has been a precious place of prayer, not only for people with handicaps, but for countless assistants and an endless stream of visitors. As happens in such places, one *feels* the prayer that has been offered there: as T.S. Eliot wrote in *Little Gidding*: 'You are here to kneel/ Where prayer has been valid.' Within the strongly Roman Catholic ethos in which the Sacrament is exposed, many people of other traditions and other Faiths come to pray in the oratory.

At the start of Asha Niketan in Kerala, South India, there were Hindus, Muslims and Christians in the community. Muslims do not have images of any kind in their place of worship, whereas for a Hindu, who has such a profound sense of God in all creation, every flower and stone and lamp can become the focal point of worship. Chris Sadler, who founded the community, asked the Muslim members if the place of prayer could have a light in the centre, and this was agreed. The oil lamp was placed on some stones upon which one could also put flowers. Viswanathan, who was a much valued member of the community, was a Hindu. One day he was sitting at the entrance to the place of prayer when a passer-by looking saw the stones and the flowers and turning to him, asked: 'Which God do you pray to?' Viswanathan replied: 'Which God? ... I do not know which God. ... We pray in the Light, that is all.'

In the prayer room in the Lambeth Community in London there is an open Bible, an icon of the Virgin and

Child, of Christ, or of the Trinity, depending on the liturgical season. And there is a large bowl with a towel, representing the L'Arche liturgy of the foot washing, which we celebrate in our communities on Holy Thursday.

At special moments like the death of a member of the house, there are times of prayer. Recently Elizabeth, a member of the Edinburgh community, died very suddenly. She was a person of great vitality and wit, totally in charge of her house, the scourge of new assistants, who routinely experienced the sharp edge of her tongue (unless they were good-looking young men), and the most amusing and loving of friends once she had accepted you. She died late one evening when most people in the house had gone to bed. The next day people went to their churches as usual but in the evening we had a small gathering of house members and those friends who had been closest to Elizabeth. It was held in the sitting room, where she had always been so much at home. A table was put out in the room covered by a bright cloth and a photograph of Elizabeth was placed on it. Gradually each person in the house, some with the help of an assistant, added their own particular offering to her memory: flowers, a drawing, the typewriter that Elizabeth had loved to use. Tom brought down a large crucifix from his room. We gathered quietly and sang and prayed and wept together. As we came to the end of the prayer time Tom stood up. He has a gift for finding the exact dramatic gesture needed at such a moment. He picked up the crucifix and went round the group, holding the crucifix aloft and blessing each person in turn. Each responded in their own way, crossing themselves, bowing silently or thanking Tom for the blessing.

Accompaniment, Retreats and Pilgrimages

Assistants who stay for any length of time in L'Arche receive accompaniment. That is to say, they meet at regular intervals with a trusted person, who has some knowledge of their situation without being a close colleague, to talk confidentially about any aspect of their life that they wish. They are also offered separate spiritual accompaniment and many find this valuable even where it has not been part of their own tradition and may be quite a new experience.

Assistants are also encouraged to go on retreat. These retreats take different forms. Some, on the continent for instance, are held in largely Roman Catholic contexts (though open, of course, to those of other traditions) while, more widely, others are inter-denominational, or, as in India, are Inter-Faith. Such times can be very powerful, particularly for young people for whom a retreat is a completely new experience.

L'Arche also offers accompaniment and retreats to core members and this has been developed in the

Lambeth Community particularly. Chris Sadler describes the 'Emmaus retreats' in which:

> 'several pairs of pilgrims, one of whom is learning disabled, spend several days together. During this retreat there are shared liturgies and other events using mime, stories, symbolic acts, but the two pilgrims in each pair also spend time alone, praying together and sharing their experience in verbal and non-verbal ways - such as through painting, modelling, or observing nature together. This is always a deeply moving and enriching experience for those who participate...Liam, who conventionally would be described as quite severely autistic, his few sounds virtually indecipherable, once drew a sequence of the pictures of the story of Zacchaeus that I had told earlier. In the first Zacchaeus was alone, out on a branch; the sun was black; Jesus was far away, almost smothered by the crowd. In the second, Jesus was close to the tree, he had become very large, as if looking eye to eye at the figure on the branch, the crowd fading away; the sun was round, yellow. In the third picture, Jesus and Zacchaeus, now both on the ground, are standing together; Jesus is not so big and Zacchaeus not so small and they turn towards the people; there are birds in the trees and others flying in the sky; the

> sun has rays radiating in all directions... I am ashamed to admit that at the time I had no idea that Liam had understood this story so deeply. He brought it alive for me in a totally new way. He, too, seemed more at peace in himself and at peace in the group when we met together again later.' (*'Accompanying people with learning disabilities'* in *Retreats 2001:6-7*)

Many communities have established a tradition of going on pilgrimage. Most have some kind of 'community journey' each year, when they celebrate their own special history. Some years ago, for example, the Liverpool community made the long and complicated journey to the island of Iona, off the west coast of Scotland. They had their own programme but they also shared in many of the Iona Community's activities, including the pilgrimage round the island, which recapitulates the story of St Columba and his followers.

A life that is shared

The Edinburgh community, prompted by its pastoral team of priests and ministers, have been considering the spiritual life of the community and more especially the place of the Eucharist within it. A discussion on the topic was held at one of the houses recently involving everyone present with the help of symbols and pictures. It was a good discussion but inevitably dominated by those who were more inclined to verbal modes of expression. Afterwards the visitors all stayed on for the evening meal. It was Wednesday, so the meal was special, there was wine on the table and the candle was lit. As we held hands round the table, a loud and cheerful grace was sung. At first the conversation was with the visitors - talk of travel and holidays and mutual friends - while most of those who belonged to the house got on with eating in silence, not because anyone felt left out but because where there is food one's first duty is to enjoy it. When everyone had eaten their first course there was a pause and in a few moments the balance of relationships round the table had changed totally, thanks to Gordon. Gordon has few words but great social gifts and he is a tremendous entertainer with a great repertoire of sounds and signs. He imitated a cat, then a donkey, then a series of birds; Tom immediately became involved in the joke, and suddenly the whole table was united in laughter and exchanges of looks and smiles and sounds that communicated at a level deeper than the words we had been using.

Almost everyone at this table has known loss, in some cases traumatic loss, of some one close and deeply loved. One at least is frequently in pain, some have physical as well as learning disabilities. Some are subject to frustration, incomprehension and outbursts of anger. Like all L'Arche houses, it is a home 'inspired by love and anger, disturbed by need and pain', yet it is at the same time a place of laughter, which is the sign of hope.

We had talked in our meeting of the unity we experienced at our meals, the table fellowship which is central to L'Arche and the sense of Our Lord's presence in its midst. As we looked round at one another I think we all knew that this supper table was indeed a celebration and a realisation of that unity. It is in the ordinary and the everyday that we find the Kingdom.

APPENDIX 1 - CONTACT DETAILS

L'Arche UK website:
www.larche.org.uk

General Enquiries
L'Arche, 10 Briggate,
Silsden, Keighley,
West Yorkshire BD20 9JT
Tel: 01535 656186
Fax: 01535 656426
E-mail: info@larche.org.uk

L'Arche Kent
Little Ewell, Barfrestone,
Dover, Kent CT15 7JJ
Tel: 01304 830930
Fax: 01304 832393
E-mail: kent@larche.co.uk

L'Arche Inverness
13 Drummond Crescent,
Inverness IV2 4QR
Tel: 01463 239615
Fax: 01463 711089
E-mail: inverness@larche.org.uk

L'Arche Liverpool
The Ark, Lockerby Road,
Liverpool L6 0HG
Tel: 0151 260 0422
Fax: 0151 263 2260
E-mail: liverpool@larche.org.uk

L'Arche Lambeth
15 Norwood High Street,
London SE27 9JU
Tel: 020 8670 6714
Fax: 020 8670 0818
E-mail: lambeth@larche.org.uk

L'Arche Bognor Regis
Bradbury House,
51a Aldwick Road,
Bognor Regis,
West Sussex PO21 2NJ
Tel: 01243 863426
Fax: 01243 840383
E-mail: bognor@larche.org.uk

L'Arche Brecon
PAVO, Steeple House,
Steeple Lane, Brecon,
Powys LD3 7DJ
Tel: 01874 624483
Fax: 01874 610046
E-mail: brecon@larche.org.uk

L'Arche Edinburgh
132 Constitution Street, Leith,
Edinburgh EH6 6AJ
Tel: 0131 553 3478
Fax: 0131 554 3236
E-mail: edinburgh@larche.org.uk

L'Arche Preston
3 Moor Park Avenue,
Preston PR1 6AS
Tel/fax: 01772 251113
E-mail: preston@larche.org.uk

Northern Ireland:

L'Arche Belfast
Floor 6, 1-3 Brunswick Street,
Belfast BT2 7GE
Tel: 028 90 596673
Fax: 028 90 872992
E-mail: bel@larche.ie

Republic of Ireland:

L'Arche Secrétariat,
Senior House, All Hallows College, Grace Park Road,
Drumcondra, Dublin 9
Tel: (International prefix from UK is 00 353) - (0)1 837 3785
Fax: (0)1 837 4379
Website: www.larche.ie

L'Arche Cork
'Le Cheile', Togher, Cork 4
Tel: (0)21 31 8880
Fax: (0)21 31 8883

L'Arche Dublin
Seolta, Warrenhouse Road,
Baldoyle, Dublin 13
Tel: (0)1 839 4356
Fax: (0)1 839 5460

L'Arche Kilkenny
'Cluain Aoibhinn',
Fair Green Lane, Callan,
Co. Kilkenny
Tel: (0)56 256 28
Fax: (0)56 259 46
E-mail: larche@iol.ir

L'Arche International:

14 rue d'Assas - 75006 Paris
Tel: (International prefix from UK is 00 33) (0)1 44 39 48 32
Fax: (0)1 44 39 48 33
E-mail: larche.internationale @wanadoo.fr

Further Reading

Many books have been written about L'Arche, and what follows is just a selection. A full list of publications, including audio and video-tapes, is available from the Silsden office above.

By Jean Vanier:

An Ark for the Poor (the story of L'Arche), published by Novalis / Geoffrey Chapman;

Community & Growth, published by Darton, Longman & Todd;

The Heart of L'Arche (spirituality for every day), published by Novalis / Geoffrey Chapman.

By Henri Nouwen:

The Road to Daybreak, published by Darton, Longman & Todd;

Bread for the Journey, published by Darton, Longman & Todd;

Letters to Marc about Jesus, published by Darton, Longman & Todd.

By other Authors:

Jean Vanier & L'Arche, by Kathryn Spink, published by Darton, Longman & Todd;

Encounter with Mystery, edited by Frances Young, published by Darton, Longman & Todd;

A Prophetic Cry, edited by Tim Kearney, published by Veritas;

Becoming Human, published by Darton, Longman & Todd 1999;

Adam, published by Darton, Longman & Todd;

Nick: Man of the Heart, by Therese Vanier, published by Gill and Macmillan 1993;
Ecumenism in L'Arche Book 1, published by International Council of L'Arche;
Ecumenism in L'Arche Book 2, published by International Council of L'Arche;
Letters of L'Arche, published quarterly by the International Federation of L'Arche and available by annual subscription.

Titles marked with an asterisk are available from the L'Arche Secretariat, 10 Briggate, Silsden, Keighley, West Yorkshire BD20 9JT.

In the UK, L'Arche is a registered charity, No. 264166, and a company limited by guarantee, registered in England & Wales, No 1055041.

APPENDIX 2 - THE CHARTER OF L'ARCHE

L'Arche began in 1964 when Jean Vanier and Father Thomas Philippe, in response to a call from God, invited RaphaÎl Simi and Philippe Seux, two men with learning disabilities, to come and share their life in the spirit of the Gospel and of the Beatitudes that Jesus preached.

From this first community, born in France and in the Roman Catholic tradition, many other communities have developed in various cultural and religious traditions.

These communities, called into being by God, are united by the same vision and the same spirit of welcome, of sharing and simplicity.

I. Aims

1. The aim of L'Arche is to create communities which welcome people with learning disabilities. By this means L'Arche seeks to respond to the distress of those who are too often rejected, and to give them a valid place in society.

2. L'Arche seeks to reveal the particular gifts of people with learning disabilities who belong at the very heart of their communities and who call others to share their lives.

3. L'Arche knows that it cannot welcome everyone who has a learning disability. It seeks to offer not a solution

but a sign, a sign that a society, to be truly human, must be founded on welcome and respect for the weak and the downtrodden.

4. In a divided world, L'Arche wants to be a sign of hope. Its communities, founded on covenant relationships between people of differing intellectual capacity, social origin, religion and culture, seek to be a sign of unity, faithfulness and reconciliation.

II. Fundamental principles

1. Whatever their gifts or their limitations, people are all bound together in a common humanity. Everyone is of unique and sacred value, and everyone has the same dignity and the same rights. The fundamental rights of each person include the rights to life, to care, to a home, to education and to work. Also, since the deepest need of a human being is to love and to be loved, each person has a right to friendship, to communion and to a spiritual life.

2. If human beings are to develop their abilities and talents to the full, realising all their potential as individuals, they need an environment that fosters personal growth. They need to form relationships with others within families and communities. They need to live in an atmosphere of trust, security and mutual affection. They need to be valued, accepted and supported in real and warm relationships.

3. People with learning disabilities often possess qualities of welcome, wonderment, spontaneity and directness. They are able to touch hearts and to call others to unity through their simplicity and vulnerability. In this way they are a living reminder to the wider world of the essential values of the heart without which knowledge, power and action lose their meaning and purpose.

4. Weakness and vulnerability in a person, far from being an obstacle to union with God, can foster it. It is often through weakness, recognised and accepted, that the liberating love of God is revealed.

5. In order to develop the inner freedom to which all people are called, and to grow in union with God, each person needs to have the opportunity of being rooted and nourished in a religious tradition.

III. The Communities

1. Communities of faith

1.1 L'Arche communities are communities of faith, rooted in prayer and trust in God. They seek to be guided by God and by their weakest members, through whom God's presence is revealed. Each community member is encouraged to discover and deepen his or her spiritual life and live it according to his or her particular faith and tradition. Those who have no religious affiliation are also welcomed and respected in their freedom of conscience.

1.2 Communities are either of one faith or inter-religious. Those which are Christian are either of one church or inter-denominational. Each community maintains links with the appropriate religious authorities and its members are integrated with local churches or other places of worship.

1.3 Communities recognise that they have an ecumenical vocation and a mission to work for unity.

2. Called to unity

2.1 Unity is founded on the covenant of love to which God calls all the community members. This implies welcome and respect for differences. Such unity presupposes that the person with a learning disability is at the centre of community life.

This unity is built up over time and through faithfulness. Communities commit themselves to accompany their members (once their membership is confirmed) throughout their lives, if this is what those members want.

2.2 Home life is at the heart of a L'Arche community. The different members of a community are called to be one body. They live, work, pray and celebrate together, sharing their joys and their suffering and forgiving each other, as in a family. They have a simple life-style which gives priority to relationships.

2.3 The same sense of communion unites the various communities throughout the world. Bound together by solidarity and mutual commitment, they form a worldwide family.

3. Called to growth

3.1 L'Arche communities are places of hope. Each person according to his or her own vocation, is encouraged to grow in love, self-giving and wholeness, as well as in independence, competence and the ability to make choices.

3.2 The communities wish to secure for their members education, work and therapeutic activities which will be a source of dignity, growth and fulfilment for them.

3.3 The communities wish to provide their members with the means to develop their spiritual life and deepen their union with and love of God and other people.

3.4 All community members are invited to participate, as far as possible, in decisions concerning them.

4. Integrated in society

4.1 L'Arche communities are open and welcoming to the world around them. They form an integral part of life in their localities, and seek to foster relationships with neighbours and friends.

4.2 The communities seek to be competent in all tasks they are called to accomplish.

4.3 The communities wish to enable people with learning disabilities to work, believing work to be an important means of integration.

4.4 The communities seek to work closely with:

- the families and guardians of people with learning disabilities,
- professionals,
- government authorities,
- and with all those who work in a spirit of justice and peace for people who have learning disabilities.

IV. Conclusion

L'Arche is deeply concerned with the distress of people who suffer injustice and rejection because they have learning disabilities. This concern should impel the communities of L'Arche to do all they can to defend the rights of people with learning disabilities, to support the creation of places of welcome for them, and to call on our society to become more just and respectful towards them.

The communities of L'Arche want to be in solidarity with the poor of the world, and with all those who take part in the struggle for justice.

Adopted by the General Assembly of the Federation of L'Arche, Cap Rouge, Quebec, May 1993.

CTS
MEMBERSHIP

We hope you have enjoyed reading this booklet. If you would like to read more of our booklets or find out more about CTS - why not do one of the following?

1. Join our Readers CLUB.
We will send you a copy of every new booklet we publish, - through the post to your address. You'll get 20% off the price too.

2. Support our work and Mission.
Become a CTS Member. Every penny you give will help spread the faith throughout the world. What's more, you'll be entitled to special offers exclusive to CTS Members.

3. Ask for our Information Pack.
Become part of the CTS Parish Network by selling CTS publications in your own parish.

Call us now on 020 7640 0042 or return this form to us at CTS, 40-46 Harleyford Road, London SE11 5AY
Fax: 020 7640 0046 email: info@cts-online.org.uk

❑ I would like to join the ***CTS Readers Club***

❑ Please send me details of how to join CTS as a ***Member***

❑ Please send me a ***CTS Information Pack***

Name:...

Address:..

....

Post Code:...

Phone:...

email address:..

Registered charity no. 218951.
Registered in England as a company limited by guarantee no.57374.